Going back

The slinx is sitting very still.
He is thinking of how to get rid of the Honkbonk.
The Honkbonk is very, very big.
If the grinlings attack him, he will just flatten them all.
The slinx must think of a trick.
He must think of something the Honkbonk is not expecting—something that will astonish him.
It is a very difficult problem.

Write

The slinx is still thinking of how to get ___ of the Honkbonk.
He thinks it is a very __________ problem.

Then, all of a sudden, the slinx thinks of a plan.
It is brilliant.
He pulls off his wellington boots.
Good!
The magnets are still there.

Draw the slinx pulling off his boots.

Write

The slinx thinks of a ____ at last.
He thinks it is __________.

The slinx jumps up and goes across to the grinlings.

He tells them that they must fix something up for him.

The grinlings rush off to collect things.

Then they come back and get on with the job as fast as they can.

Draw the grinlings getting on with the job.

Write

The grinlings have to ________ some things.

At last the grinlings finish the job.
You cannot see what it is, because they have put a big blanket on top of it.
The slinx gives them a clap.
He tells them that now they must get on with the next bit of his plan.
This is the difficult bit!
The grinlings drag the thing off.
They are going to the cliff where the Honkbonk lives.

Write

Everyone sets off for the _ _ _ _ _ where the Honkbonk lives.

There is a lot of pushing and pulling, but the grinlings get there at last.

Now they are all panting and gasping, so they sit down for a rest.

The Honkbonk is down at the bottom of the cliff.

He is standing next to his prison with a big stick in his hand.

He is prodding the grinlings with the stick and yelling insults at them.

He loves to upset them.

Draw the Honkbonk prodding the grinlings.

Write

The Honkbonk prods the grinlings with his _ _ _ _ _ .

You little creeps!

Back at the top of the cliff, everyone pushes and pulls until the thing is in the exact spot.

The slinx pulls off the blanket.

Now everyone can see the thing.

It is a colossal fishing rod, resting on a big stand.

Some magnets are dangling from the end of the rod.

The slinx stands on a rock.

'Are you all ready?' he asks.

Everyone nods.

'Let it go then!' the slinx tells them.

Draw the fishing rod.

Write

The slinx pulls off the ________.

Now everyone can see that the slinx has invented a magnetic ________ rod.

Down go the magnets.

CLANK!

They hit the Honkbonk and stick fast.

Now everyone helps to pull the Honkbonk up.

Up he goes.

He is struggling and yelling.

He grabs at the magnets, but they will not come unstuck.

He goes up and up and up.

Draw the Honkbonk dangling from the magnets.

Write

The _______ stick to the Honkbonk.

Now everyone _____ him up.

Now the Honkbonk is level with the cliff top.

The Honkbonk is frantic—he can see what the slinx is going to do.

SNIP!

The Honkbonk goes tumbling back down.

CRASH! THUD! SLAM! CRACK!

There is nothing left of the Honkbonk, just bits of scrap metal, nuts, cogs, buttons and springs.

Draw the Honkbonk hitting the bottom of the cliff.

Write

The Honkbonk crashes down to the bottom of the cliff and smashes into ____.

CRASH!
THUD!

Now they have got rid of the Honkbonk, everyone is happy.

Some of the grinlings dash down to the bottom of the cliff.

One of them unlocks the prison and the rest of them pick up the bits of the Honkbonk.

Then they all set off back.

Draw the grinlings getting out of prison.

Write

The grinlings are happy to get out of ______.

Everyone has a good sleep, then one of the grinlings comes to see the slinx.

He tells the slinx that they will help him to mend his rocket.

They will do the best they can.

The slinx jumps up.

He is very happy.

'Come on, then!' he yells.

Write

The grinlings are going to ____ the rocket.

The grinlings get cracking.
They patch up the rocket with bits from the Honkbonk.
They do a very good job.
In the end, everything is ready.
'What do you think of the rocket now?' they ask the slinx.
But the slinx is sad.
He had forgotten that the rocket had run out of petrol.

Write

The grinlings _____ up the rocket with bits from the Honkbonk.
But the slinx still has a problem.
The rocket has run out of
______.

Everyone is glum.
Then some of the grinlings pull the two gas tanks out of the rocket.
'What are these?' they ask.
The slinx tells them that the tanks are full of gas.
'That is splendid!' yells one of the grinlings, and he does a little jig.
The slinx thinks that this is very puzzling.

Write

One of the grinlings thinks he can do something with the

___ ______.

gas

The grinling tells the rest of them what to do.

Now they attach the gas tanks to the rocket.

They fix two plugs to the bottom of the tanks, then they fix some string to the plugs.

The slinx is ready to set off, but he can see that the grinlings are sad to see him go.

He gives them all a hug, and thanks them for helping him.

Then he gets into the rocket, and locks up the hatch.

Draw the slinx hugging one of the grinlings.

Write

The grinlings are ___ to see him go.

The grinlings pull the string.
The plugs drop out.

HISS!

The gas gushes out.

SWISH!

The rocket lifts off.
The slinx is going back!
He intends to land the rocket on his dump.
That will give the fuzzbuzzes a shock!

Write

The rocket _____ off.

The slinx will land on his dump and give the fuzzbuzzes a _____.

But it is the slinx that gets the shock.

He does not have a soft landing.

The rocket hits the dump with a terrific crash and then it splits into two.

The slinx comes tumbling out.

The fuzzbuzzes dash across to see what is happening.

The fuzzbuzzes are sad to see the slinx in such a mess.
They put him on the mattress under the apple tree.
They will patch him up, and let him stop there until he is well.
The slinx has lumps, bumps, cuts and scratches.
But he is grinning with happiness.
He is back at last.

1. What does the slinx wish he had? (4)
2. What does the Honkbonk do with his stick? (10)
3. What does the Honkbonk yell at the grinlings in his prison? (11)
4. What has the slinx invented? (12)
5. What happens to the Honkbonk? (16)
6. What has the slinx forgotten? (22)
7. What do the grinlings fix to the bottom of the gas tanks? (26)
8. Where does the slinx intend to land? (28)
9. What happens to the rocket? (30)
10. Where do the fuzzbuzzes put the slinx? (31)